HOW
GUITAR
FOR KIDS

The little handbook

By

M DIBLEY

Thanks for purchasing this book, so you either have a guitar or are thinking about getting one, well lucky for you this book will be able to point you in the right direction, you don't need any previous musical knowledge as we'll delve into the basics and a bit of music theory, how to play songs, techniques and chords and of course a lot, lot more.

So once again thanks for purchasing this book and please read on.

Contents

Introduction 1
Guitar Tuning 3
Music Notes 4
Guitar Accessories & Pedals 6
Learning your first song 12
Guitar Picking 16
Guitar Chords 18
Guitar Warm Up Exercises 22
Useful Techniques Beginners Should Know 31
Commonly asked questions 39
Time Signatures 42
Chord Progressions 44

INTRODUCTION

So, you've either just bought a guitar or picked it up for the very first time and you're looking at the body, looking at the strings and the neck and you are feeling very confused!

Well, let me break it down for you. If it's an electric guitar, the body is where the electric parts are held.

or if it's acoustic you will see a hole and that's what the sound resonates into.

The neck, as you see, will have fret markers or numbers on them and they just give you a guideline to what fret number you're playing on.

The picture below for example has fret markers that start on the 3rd fret and end on the 21st fret. It's true some guitars do have more frets than others but don't let that bother you its just the design of the guitar.

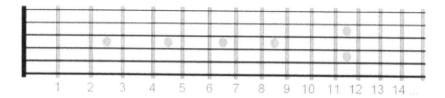

Each time you hold down a certain fret, the notes will change and depending on the notes you are holding down will make up the chord pattern. For example, if you were to locate the notes C E G on the fretboard and hold them down together this would make up a C Major scale. Why? You might ask, we will get to that a bit later on.

GUITAR TUNING

So, it's time to play!

Make sure you've tuned your guitar to the standard guitar tuning the 6th string, which is the thickest, and is at the bottom, and the 1st string is the thinnest, which is located at the top. Each string represents a different note. These notes are as follows

E A D G B E

You can make up any abbreviation or acronym for this, a popular one to remember is "**E**ddie **A**te **D**ynamite **G**ood **B**ye **E**ddie"

If you haven't tuned your guitar yet, buy a guitar tuner, preferably a clip on one as it is less hassle for a beginner, turn it on and pluck one string at a time. On the top of the neck of the guitar you get things called machine heads or tuners you will see three of these on each side of the guitars head. To alternate between the different notes, you will need twist the tuning pegs either clockwise or anti- clockwise. Which way you twist the peg depends on whether you are changing one note to one higher up or lower down. To tune an 'E' note to a 'G' note, you would need to turn the pegs anti-clockwise, because the note is below the original. To change an 'E' note to a 'B', you would need to turn the peg clockwise.

This is not stating for all cases as you can set the tuning anti clockwise and make it go higher in pitch rather than lower but commonly you will find this rule applies.

To know you've got the right note make sure you stop tuning it when your tuner normally turns green or a different colour than what the flats or sharps are giving off on the tuner.

MUSIC NOTES

So, let's look at every single note in music;

There are 12 notes in music and they are...
A, A#, B, C, C#, D, D#, E, F, F#, G, G#,

So, you're probably thinking what the hash signs mean? And where is B# and E#?

Well the hash signs stand for 'sharp', the highest note before it reaches the next note.

And there is no B# or E# in music. The notes simply do not exist.

It might be worth remembering the notes I wrote out for you could also be written like this;

Ab, A, Bb, B, C, Db, D, Eb, E, F, Gb, G

So why could it be written out like this?

Because flats and sharps are the same note just the sharp is the highest of the note and the flat is the lowest pitch of the note, so a 'Gb' is the same as an 'F#' and an 'A#' is the same as a 'Bb'.

\#-SHARP
b- FLAT

So now you know when tuning your guitar if you need to get to the note 'E' if the note is lower you will have to turn the tuners clockwise and obviously anti clockwise for a lower note.

You must be careful to pay attention and not tune to fast or hard as the string could snap!

Okay, so now you've tuned your guitar, the next chapter i'll talk about some guitar accessories and pedals.

GUITAR ACCESSORIES & PEDALS

As a new guitar player you're at a stage to where you're intrigued by what is it that makes that sound on that song you know and love.

I am going to post some examples below of some accessories you can get for your guitar.

Bottle Neck - You place this on your finger and you use this to slide along the frets creating a country/blues sound. You can get different types of bottle necks.

Glass Bottleneck

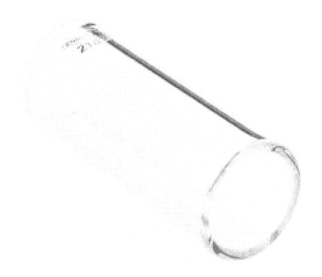

Steel Bottleneck

Brass Bottleneck

The cost of bottle necks, luckily, they are affordable and cheap they range typically between £5-£10 (approx $7-$12)

E-bow - This strange yet authentic sounding accessory is one for the experimentalist. The E-bow can be found in a lot of songs. The most famous ones would be U2 With or Without You (that high-pitched sound that sounds like a violin in the background) The Church - Under the Milky Way (Solo) and REM - E-bow The Letter. I prefer using an E-bow for added texture/weight in a song. E-Bows have on option to where you can switch between making your guitar sounding like a violin to making your guitar sound like a cello.

SO HOW DOES IT WORK?

The E-bow is powered by a battery which drives a magnetic field which bends the guitar string.

HOW DO YOU PLAY ONE?

The E-bow is positioned between your finger and thumb, you'll notice on the underneath there are 2 groves these will fit on the guitar strings and the middle of the E-bow will be creating the magnetic field and bending the string in between.

The cost of an E bow is just under £100 (Approx $100) picture is below

GUITAR PEDALS

Distortion Pedal - A distortion pedal works by applying an increase in gain, this is the pedal that creates an increase in gain and creates a very heavy sound one popular with the heavy metal genre.

Overdrive Pedal - Overdrive generates less amount of tone change than distortion. Overdrive will be better if you want a cleaner sound. It's main purpose is to mimic the volume button on your amp but is a far safer and neighbour friendly option.

Fuzz Pedal - Fuzz pedal is a style of compressed distortion; it alters the waveform and clips the signal to bring about the fuzz sound. Bands like Dinosaur Jr & Jimi Hendrix used fuzz pedals.

Reverb Pedal - Reverb pedal is to emulate playing in a large space, the idea is to bring an echo back to the listener. There are a lot of affects you can get with reverb making the sound, sound like you're playing in a church or in a bathroom and lots more open spaces. The Beatles used their "natural reverb chamber" in abbey road.

Delay Pedal - The delay pedal will record and playback music fed into it and the playback can normally be altered in variation to create a quick or slow delay.

Echo Pedal - An Echo pedal is similar to a delay pedal but the delay is greater

Wah Wah Pedal - It is controlled by movement of the player's foot on a rocking pedal and creates a "wah" sound.

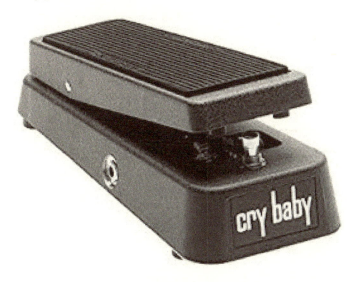

LEARNING YOUR FIRST SONG

So, you should now be ready to have a go at that song you've always wanted to play!

I'm going to post below if you know how to read tabs - Deep Purple's Smoke on the Water.

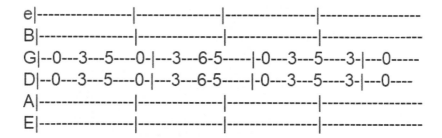

If you don't know how to read tabs just yet, then please read on…..

A useful site for guitar tabs is www.ultimate-guitar.com (they have hundreds of thousands of songs on here, make sure you click on the tab version of the song though)

Go on the site and choose a song you want to learn. Hopefully, you'll find one to your liking. There are hundreds of thousands to choose from!

Now make sure you click on the file that says 'tab'! This will be the first step for a beginner to learn how to read tabbed songs, and you will gain an understanding for your future development.

When you have a look at your first song tab, you will normally see that the lines have a letter for each string, but if that's not the case then each line represents the string as you'd be looking at the guitar.

Most of the time you will see this type of tablature.

Diagram 1

```
E-----------------
B-----------------
G-----------------
D-----------------
A-------4--------
E-----2----------
```

Or you'll see this type of tablature.

Diagram 2

```
E-------3---------------
B-------3---------------
G-------3---------------
D-------3---------------
A-------4--------------
E-------3--------------
```

So why does the first diagram have a separation of the numbers? In the second diagram why do the numbers align with one another? The answer is simple!

Diagram 1 - means you pick the notes individually

Diagram 2 - means you'll hold all the notes down together and strum/play the notes together

So, you're thinking "I can see the letters, and numbers next to the letters but what do the numbers mean?"

Take a look at your guitar neck and count each individual fret. You will see they are numbered with markers simply called "fret markers". If you count them, you will see they'll normally count to around 21 or 22 frets. Some have slightly more, which all depends on the brand of the guitar.

Diagram 1

E-------------------

B------------------

G-----------------

D-----------------

A----------4-------

E-------2---------

So, diagram 1 means go to the thickest string, the E string, sometimes called the

low E, and hold the E string down on the 2nd fret and pick the note.

Then hold down the A string on the fourth fret and pick that note, the A string is the 5th string the 2nd thickest string! You will notice a change of pitch or tone and that is because the note has changed.

Take a look at this diagram of the guitar neck and look at the relation to the notes and the numbers it's like plotting out a graph!

You might still be wondering why you see two E notes.

The answer is because one is higher or one is lower than the other.

Look at a keyboard or a piano there is a flow of different notes you have the white keys which are notes A-G and the black keys which are the sharps/flats and then the pattern continues once you reach the end note and the notes start again, but this time they're just higher notes than the last.

So, the same rules apply to the guitar each fret is its own individual note, each fret will be either higher or lower sounding depending which fret you are playing.

So, pick both E strings and you will notice one will be higher/lower than the other.

GUITAR PICKING

Some other useful things to remember or know is 'Picking', so you either get a down stroke or an up stroke depending on how the song is played, a good tip would be to gently place your first finger (index) across all the 6 strings lightly so when you go to play something no sound rings out, so block the strings from buzzing basically, and practice your down strokes and upstrokes and change the rhythm around by maybe doing one upstroke then two down strokes and vice versa. There are plenty of videos on 'Youtube' that could tell you how to do this if you're still unsure.

Normally typing in 'strumming for beginners' sets you along the right path.

I will now show you what an upstroke and a down stroke looks like in music notation. You might see some people do the symbols differently in tabbed versions. Follow what they put, by all means, but just remember their version is technically the wrong version!

⊓ = Downstroke

V = Upstroke

✘ = Mute

A way to remember these symbols would be to think about the direction of these symbols. The symbols actually depict the opposite of its actual description. Strangely enough the simple for the upstroke looks like it's pointing down and the symbol for the down stroke looks like it's pointing up when it's really vice versa, so remember the opposite applies!

Refer back to this diagram if you ever forget.

You have to remember whoever it was that influenced you to play the guitar they were once a beginner guitarist like you, they were not born with a guitar at hand. It was something that they played over and over again to be the well-known guitarist that they are today!

So in the last segment we left off at what a guitar tab is and how to read them.

Now let's start off at another important point! And that's reading guitar chords.

GUITAR CHORDS

So, what is a guitar chord? A chord technically is 3 different notes or more.

So, what do I mean? Let's take all the notes in music;
A, A#, B, C, C#, D, D#, E, F, F#, G, G#

If you were to take any of these three notes and combine them you would be creating a guitar chord.

So, in this example I am going to take the notes C, E, G, and this arrangement of notes will give me a C MAJOR CHORD.

Since we have only just begun discussing this subject, I will refrain from explaining the why's and the how's of the chord formation. If you are interested in the theory behind it I will explain why below but I don't want this to get too confusing.

This is because for any major chord you will be taking the 1st 3rd and 5th note of the major scale, it just so happens C is the 1st note E is the 2nd note and G is the 3rd note of the C Major scale.

So, I will now show you what the diagram of a C major chord looks like and I will show you what it looks like in tab form, and will relate the two for you so you can read the structure properly.

So, the C Major Chord looks like this

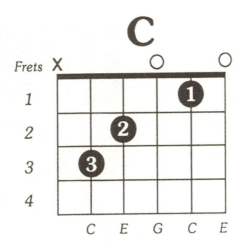

If you study both diagrams closely you should see how they correlate. If you flip the chord chart of the C Major 90 degrees anti clockwise you can see it will spell out the same as the tab below.

Notice how you see the notes 'C, E, G, C, E' at the bottom of the diagram. Well, it doesn't matter how many notes are in the chord as long as they're the same notes of C, E, G, they could be shown in any self-replicating way like..........C, G, E, C, E or G, E, C. It really doesn't matter, as long as they contain those three notes then you will have a C Major Chord!!!

HOW DO I READ THAT CHORD DIAGRAM?

It's simple. The numbers inside the circles represent your finger placements, and the vertical lines represent the strings. You will count 6 vertical lines which represent the 6 strings on the guitar.

The diagram above shows 4 horizontal lines which indicate your frets, and the bold black line at the top represents the nut of the guitar (The end of the neck of the guitar before it reaches the head).

The X you see means you do not play that string! So the first note would be the A string on the 3rd fret, the open circles you see (O) means you play the string open, which means just play the string as it is, for example, if you didn't hold any frets down and just strummed the guitar as is then the whole strings would be open!

The black dots just tell you whereabouts you play, on what fret and what string, they're like numbers plotted on a graph and your job is to decipher and match them up to what string and fret it depicts.

So now it's time to have a look at what the C Major Chord looks like in tab form.

C Major Chord

```
E-----------0-----
B----------1-------
G---------0---------
D-------2-----------
A-----3-------------
E—X--------------
```

As discussed in the first segment, the numbers represent the frets and the letters represent the strings, in tab forms they don't tell you about finger placements they're just not detailed enough and that really is the point of them! But I will tell you just for convenience.

In this chord, put your 3rd finger on the 3rd fret of the A string

Put your 2nd finger (middle finger) on the 2nd fret of the D string

Put your 1st finger (index finger) on the 1st fret of the B string.

Now look and compare the two images and see how they correlate.

This is how you will see and read chords in most forms of music today.

It might be worthwhile to note that all major chords are derived from the major scale and consist of only three different notes, so although the C major chord I have shown you above has 5 notes, there are only 3 different notes. This is because this one has five. It is just to make the sound bigger/more powerful and is the most common C Major chord, one of the most important thing is not to get restricted in your playing. That's why information is key, the more information you have the more you can deal with.

Our next topic we will move onto will be some guitar warm up exercises.

GUITAR WARM UP EXERCISES

Now as a beginner I remember how hard it was to try and get fluidity in my playing.

When I first started playing, I remember that my fingers and my hands were so sore. Sore enough that it can be compared to after workout sores. Some chords ask you to contort your fingers and use your fingers in a way that we have never used them before. That's why the instrument feels alien when we first start. Our tendons and muscles in the palms of our hands can feel sore and tight too.

Callouses can also make it painful. Remember, don't play until you bleed!

Despite what all the stupid songs say, if you play until you bleed it means the longer you have to rest and that's more hours you have to rest and not play the guitar.

So, a good exercise to do is to try and move your fingers across all the frets. The reason why this is such a good method is because it allows your brain to have a relation between fret spacing and finger adjustment, as you'll notice the frets get smaller the higher up the fret board it is.

At first you will find it extremely difficult to move some of your fingers. I know a lot of people struggle with moving their little finger, as it doesn't really get used much in many day to day activities so trying to train it with your other fingers might seem alien at first but it's something that's important in guitar playing.

So, let's take a look at the guitar exercise. I will show this for you in tab form, we will basically be playing a chromatic scale and you may ask 'what is a chromatic scale?'

Well, a chromatic scale is a musical scale that has twelve pitches, each a semitone or half step apart. In simple terms, a scale in which you'll be playing all the 12 notes in music, which are as follows;

A, A#, B, C, C#, D, D#, E, F, F#, G, G#

So, here is the tab for it

```
E-------------------------------------------------1-2-3-4
B-----------------------------------------1-2-3-4----------
G---------------------------------1-2-3-4--------------------
D-----------------------1-2-3-4------------------------------
A------------1-2-3-4-----------------------------------------
E-1-2-3-4----------------------------------------------------
```

You must remember to try to use all four fingers to do this. Try not to just use one finger. This exercise is to really get the fret board and your fingers correlating.

And once you get to the end of the scale, work your way down from it like so..............

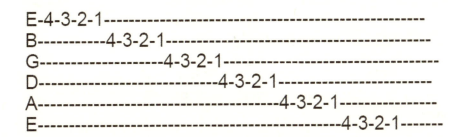

```
E-4-3-2-1----------------------------------------------------
B-----------4-3-2-1-------------------------------------------
G-------------------4-3-2-1-----------------------------------
D-----------------------------4-3-2-1-------------------------
A-------------------------------------4-3-2-1-----------------
E-----------------------------------------------4-3-2-1-------
```

You can play these notes anywhere. The best thing to do is to try to cover as much of the fret board as possible. You can try to get up to the twelfth fret at least.

Guitar exercises are very undervalued! Even a lot of the great guitarists don't do them, or so they say, but once you keep practicing these, you will soon see massive changes in your playing.

On one last note, it might be worth alternating your picking when doing the warm up exercises, so maybe do it in a pattern of down stroke one note, then upstroke the other, spice things up a little bit—any practice is good practice after all!

Okay, so in the previous segment we had a look at some guitar warm up exercises and I showed you the chromatic scale, now it's time to delve deeper into scales.

So why should any guitarist learn a scale?

A guitar scale is where you will learn to improvise and learn how to do solos.

Any guitar solo is a handful of notes taken from a scale, most times unintentionally as most guitar players don't know many guitar scales and, although they improvise over the rhythm, most guitar players probably wouldn't be able to tell you what scale they're playing from.

To cut a long story short, it's like getting a singer who can sing but they don't know what note it is they're singing, they can just hear it.

The Minor Pentatonic Scale

So, the guitar scale we're going to look at is the minor pentatonic scale, this is the scale that most guitar players use and improvise over.

Why, you ask? Well, it is a very easy scale that doesn't require much finger usage as it only contains 5 different notes (think Pent or Pentagon which has 5 sides) and it forms the basis of most blues and rock improvisation.

One last important thing to mention is to do the scale slowly at first, I know you're probably thinking that you see your favourite guitar player shred it, but anything new we must approach with a process, just as when we were babies we weren't expected to crawl when we first came out, everything has a learning process even if we don't realise it.

So, let's take a look at the G minor pentatonic scale.

Remember to look at the diagram carefully, the number 3 outside the box represents the fret number, and the numbers inside the circles represent your finger placements.

I know some people struggle to play with their 'pinky', or little finger, at first, but if you can get used to playing it with your little finger, you'll be skipping classes a lot quicker so to speak.

It's probably best to work your way all the way up then all the way down just to get your fingers used to playing it backwards, which, if you can't understand, I'll show you in the diagram below.

G Minor Pentatonic Diagram

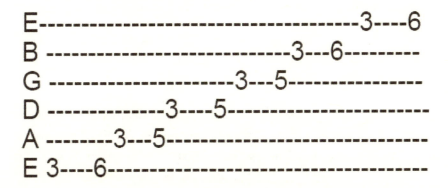

So, this is what the scale looks like if you see it in tab form. So, if you're still having trouble seeing the relation between tab versions and the proper scale structure diagrams then just compare the two shown above!

And this is what the scale looks like if you are coming down the scale.

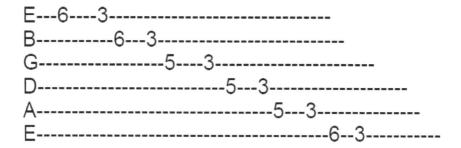

So, practice these scales, they're both exactly the same just this one you're working you way down from top to bottom instead of bottom to top.

Now time to briefly get into why this is a G minor pentatonic scale.

The reason is because it is in the shape of a minor pentatonic scale but, most importantly, it starts on the G root note. So, remember, in chapter 1 I told you that each time you hold down a fret it changes the note you're playing. Well, it just so happens that, if you were to hold down the 3rd fret of the Low E string (the thickest string), that note would no longer be E but it would be G, hence why that is a G minor pentatonic scale.

Now, if you were to keep the pattern the same as the G minor scale but moved it across 2 frets it would become an A minor pentatonic scale. As the note A is 2 notes away from G, in between those notes is, of course, G# and then you get A.

So, let me quickly show you what the A minor pentatonic scale looks like, remember it's the same shape as the G minor pentatonic but just moved across 2 frets.

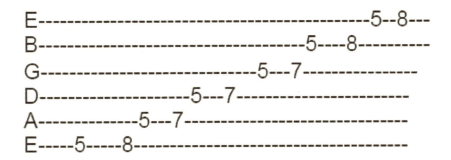

It's probably worth noting that you cannot move this shape to a higher string, this scale would then become redundant and would no longer be minor pentatonic. Minor pentatonic scales can have different patterns though, of course, but this very pattern I am showing you is the common one that most guitar players use. You can, however, move this shape across frets and it will still be a minor pentatonic; the root note you start on determines which minor pentatonic scale it is.

If you listen to the band ACDC songs, or Oasis and thousands of other guitarists, they all use these minor pentatonic scales a lot of the time.

Just keep practising these patterns and you will become faster and faster just like that guitar player you always wanted to be.

The Root Note

So, you heard me talk about the root note quite a bit in previous pages and you're wondering what is a root note?

Well, a root note is the starting note and is used as the foundation to build a scale or a chord.

Notice in the last section where I showed you the minor pentatonic scale and I showed you two variations—one was the G minor pentatonic and the other was the A minor pentatonic scale. As explained earlier, they were given those names because of the root note (the note of the first string) they started on. For example, the note on the first fret of the low E string is named F. Well, it just happens that, if you kept the same minor pentatonic shape and moved it to the first fret you would be playing an F minor pentatonic, it really is as simple as that!

Every beginner starts out with number systems, it is a good stepping tool, and then as we progress, we can then move on to the real system, which a lot of guitarists really aren't that familiar with. But as expressed in the last chapter, the more information we have to deal with the easier things become.

So, going back to the very first chapter you will see I gave you a list of 12 notes, now don't worry if you can't remember them, I will show you again.

So, the easiest thing to remember is there is no B# OR E#; this can also be expressed as there is no Cb and Fb— remember, sharps and flats are the same thing!

So now we have that out of the way let's start counting those 12 notes.

A, A#, B, C, C#, D, D#, E, F, F#, G, G#

Keep in mind that each fret represents a note so you can use these notes to remember what comes after the note you may be playing.

So, ask yourself why is the note G on the 3rd fret?

Well, look at the 12 notes I have just given, we know the E string is the open string, don't we? So, count 3 notes on from E and look at what note arrives, it is the G note.

And that is why the G minor pentatonic scale starts on the 3rd fret.

If you're still unconvinced, let's take a look at the G major chord.

I will show you the chord diagram and tabbed version; have a look at where the note starts.

Can you see the G note? The 3rd fret of the first string—look at the notes listed in the diagram. Remember the first chapter where I told you all major chords only have 3 different notes? Well, just take a look, you can see the notes are three notes which are G, B and D.

The tabbed version of the G major chord looks like this, the only reason why I still show you the tabbed version is just for extra familiarisation.

E—3-

B—0-

G—0-

D—0-

A—2-

E—3-

Just in case you still don't quite get it, remember the A minor pentatonic scale I showed you and how that started on the fifth fret of the low E string?

Well, take a look at the 12 notes again:
A, A#, B, C, C#, D, D#, E, F, F#, G, G#

Count five notes on from the letter E and you will arrive at A. Now let's look at the A major chord.

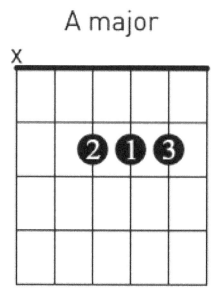

Now look at the notes of the A major chord, and look at the very first note, hopefully you can see that it's A. Remember about the three different notes I told you every major chord has? Well, just look at the notes this chord contains... A, C#, E.

Now, although the scale note of the A minor pentatonic was on the bottom string of the fifth fret, the A string is also found on the fifth string, the second thickest string if you play it open as the guitar standard tuning is

E, A, D, G, B, E

Now, before we leave for Chapter 4, let's look at some useful techniques beginners should know.

USEFUL TECHNIQUES BEGINNERS SHOULD KNOW

What's a Hammer on?

A hammer on is you hold one note down and with one of your fingers you simply hammer on to the next note. So, hold down the G string of the 3rd fret and hammer onto the fifth fret, you don't pick any notes you just hammer the note shortly after you picked the first note................ pick the note then hammer on, there's many videos on YouTube which can show you if you still can't understand.

What's a Pull Off?

A pull off is the reverse of a hammer on, so put your first finger on the 1st fret of the low E string and your third finger on the 3rd fret of the low E string and pick the note whilst sweeping away your third finger and still keeping your first finger on there. Once again, there's many videos which will show you how to do it.

So now we're up to part 4, it is time to delve into a few more guitar techniques and then on to some chords.

Other Guitar Techniques

So, we ended part 3 on what a hammer on is and what a pull of is, now I will show you what the symbols for those look like below.

These are probably some of the easiest symbols to remember as well.

H- HAMMER ON

P- PULL OFF

Now I will show you an example of where they might be used.

Let's do something basic. So, if we were to look at a tab, for example, and you needed to hammer on from the 5th fret of the high E string to the 7th fret of the high E string what would that look like in writing?

```
         H
E------5------7
B---------------
G---------------
D---------------
A---------------
E---------------
```

So the diagram just lets you know where to hammer on—easy!

Now let's look at a pull off and the diagram of that.

```
         P
E--7-------5-------------
B------------------------
G------------------------
D------------------------
A------------------------
E------------------------
```

And, last but not least, let's take a look at a trill. What's a trill? Simply, a trill is a combination of a hammer on and a pull off but you just repeat them like this: H P H P H P H P

But instead of writing it like this, you just see it like this: tr You might see it sometimes like this: tr ~~~~

It doesn't really matter, as long as it contains the tr you know exactly what it means.

Let's take a look at an example of a trill.

```
       tr tr  tr   tr   tr  tr  tr
    E --5-6--5--6--5--6--5--6
    B------------------------
    G------------------------
    D------------------------
    A------------------------
    E------------------------
```

You might see the tr sometimes beside the numbers but it means the same thing!

Let's take a look at the most commonly used technique and that is bending.

Now I know you may be thinking 'What is the point of these techniques, I will probably never use them"? but there are a lot of songs that do use them and string bending is quite popular amongst soloists. Now, if you want to be a rhythm player then you probably don't need to know this unless you want to bend some chords which that in itself has it's own time and place.

So how do you perform string bending? Simple, hold down a string and pick it. Now, whilst holding it down, move it up or down in a bending motion and you will hear the sound start to change. Whether you do a half bend or whole bend all depends how far you bend the string; obviously a whole bend changes the note by a whole note and a half bend changes the note by half a tone.

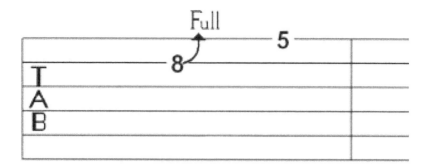

So, this is a diagram of string bending, simple really! Look at the arrows; you basically copy the texture of the arrow definition and, with a bit of practice, you'll get it. Remember, if you bend the string too far there is a risk of it snapping and a risk of injury, so just be aware!

Now the technique part is over, it's time to get some insight. So many times, you get asked who's the best guitar player in the world and then you hear hours' worth of pointless squabbling as if it's a fact when it's a subjective answer.

There never has been the best guitar player in the world, sure, some are better than others due to either longer playing, more hours practiced or wanting to learn more, but any instrument is something to learn for life, you can never master it. Someone may be a speed player but they may not be a chord master and vice versa, or you may have all the technique down but you can't play country or you can't play jazz, this is why the best guitar player in the world doesn't exist. There are always new outlets, new things to conquer.

I felt like I had to add that in there as I bet you have either heard or will hear this at some point in your life, so now you know, hopefully this can encourage some peace and quiet for many years to come. Eddie Van Halen is not Jimi Hendrix; Jimi Hendrix is not Eddie Van

Halen; Eric Clapton is Eric Clapton... List me any guitarist and they're different from the next one, enough said!

Major and Minor Chords

I feel we haven't touched on many chords so I will list you some major and minor chords in their open position.

Remember, with chords, major chords will either say A -G major or it will have a capital M; and minor chords won't normally say minor they'll just have a small m.

M-Major

m-minor

simple!

So I will first show you some of the major chords in their open position below.

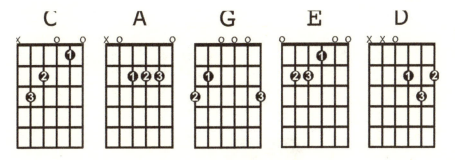

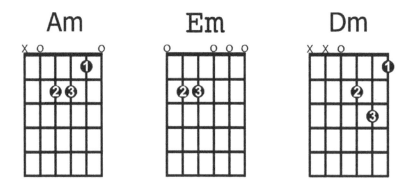

Now, with these 8 chords I have just given you, you can now play thousands and thousands of songs as you'll notice that most songs contain these chords.

Let me quickly get into chord barring for you.

So, take a look at the G minor chord, you see how you need to put your first finger across all the strings of the 3rd fret, well this technique is called barring. You need to 'barre' your finger across the whole fret.

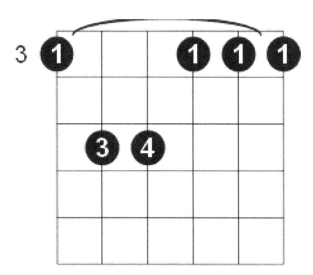

As a beginner you will probably find this difficult but practice makes perfect as the old saying goes.

There are many videos on YouTube which instruct and show you how too barre in case you have any problems in doing so.

Now we're coming to an end of sorts, you've learnt how to perform chords and read guitar tabs, you've learnt a couple of scales and you've also learnt a bit of theory of the guitar and how chords are constructed.

What is an Octave?

Now a common word you'll hear a lot in music is 'Octave'.

And you might be thinking, what is an octave? Well, an octave is the same note but higher up in the scale. Each octave has a 12-note distance between them.

Take a look at the guitar; you know that the bottom open string is E and the 12th fret of the low E string, or bottom string, is also an E note, so play both versions and there will be a difference in pitch and you will then be playing in octaves.

Take any note from the guitar and then count 12 notes along and you will reach the same note an octave higher than the previous note.

So it's time to show you a chart of all the notes on the guitar. I'll only go up to fret 12 as, after that, the notes start again, so take a look below.

e	F	F#	G	G#	A	A#	B	C	C#	D	D#	e
B	C	C#	D	D#	E	F	F#	G	G#	A	A#	B
G	G#	A	A#	B	C	C#	D	D#	E	F	F#	G
D	D#	E	F	F#	G	G#	A	A#	B	C	C#	D
A	A#	B	C	C#	D	D#	E	F	F#	G	G#	A

E	F	F#	G	G#	A	A#	B	C	C#	D	D#	E

Look at all the different notes and look at all the same notes, each one lower or higher in the scale dependant on where you're starting from/finishing at.

It's important to add that no one expects you to revise all these notes overnight, are they important? Sure, I think it's good to get past the number system but it's not important for the playing part, there are thousands upon thousands of guitarists who have made it or are even considered masters without knowing any theory at all!

Now let's take a look at one more scale and that is the major pentatonic scale.

C Major Pentatonic Scale example

Now there are other scales and positions but I think the motivation has to come from the guitar player him/herself, there's a ton of free information out there and if you want to progress then your own motivation/enthusiasm will let you do so. But this is an important scale to learn so please practice this.

Now, as a beginner guitarist I know there's probably a ton of questions you'd like to ask, so let me answer some for you, on the next page.

COMMONLY ASKED QUESTIONS

Is there a way to hold a guitar pick properly?

A: Not really. I mean most players hold it at the top with the pointy part towards the string, but whatever feels comfortable for you.

How often should I change guitar strings?

A: Well, the normal answer is every couple of weeks. Remember, most guitar strings these days are steel so there definitely are a lot of reasons for the strings to start to dull in tone, but don't worry yourselves too much as I don't know any guitarist who changes their strings that often.

Is there a difference between acoustic/electric?

A: Apart from the physical appearance and how they produce sound, there is no difference in the way they're played, they both have the same amount of strings and the tuning is the same so the transition should be a smooth one.

How often should I practice?

A: I think most people practise every day, I mean I use the term 'practise' loosely, when you really think about it practise sounds like a chore and you cannot progress at anything if it's a chore.

What is palm muting?

A: Now palm muting is something that we haven't covered or talked about in this book but it is simply placing your right hand, or lower part of it at least, on the bridge of your guitar and you will get a muted sound ring out and that's what you call palm muting!!

What are open chords?

A: Open chords are chords that have open strings in them, simple!

What are power chords?

A: Power chords are technically not chords as, if you remember from an earlier chapter, a chord is technically three different notes or more!

So, let me show you the power chord position. Tabbed Version

```
E X          E X
B X          B X
G X    OR    G 3
D 3          D 3
A 3          A 1
E 1          E X
```

You can play the same shape anywhere on the neck but only on the first two strings or lines of the fret board.

As soon as you do that position on the D string it doesn't become a power chord as the relation between the strings changes and it contains 3 different notes rather than two.

EXAMPLE E X

B X

G 7

D 7   THIS IS FINE BUT..............

A 5

E X

E X B 7

G 7

D 5 A X

E X   THIS ISN'T

Take a look back at the table of notes I gave you and you can configure exactly what notes these are.

I'll post a few power chords below for reference and instruction.

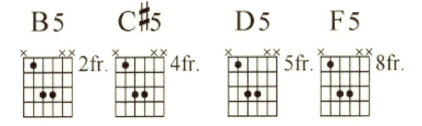

TIME SIGNATURES

Let's touch up on some things which I probably should have mentioned a bit earlier on. First let's look at time signatures and the most common time signatures that most bands use, which is 4/4 time. So, what is 4/4 time? Well 4/4 time can also be referred to as "common time" and can also be abbreviated as just "C". So, what does the first 4 represent? Well that represents how many beats there are in a bar, and in this case that's 4. And the bottom number – in this case 4 again – means what type of beat is it, so what note goes into a whole note or semibreve 4 times. Please note, whole notes and semibreves are the same thing, just whole note is the American version and semibreve is the British version.

So, going back to the number 4 we have to look at what beat is it that can fit into a semibreve or whole note 4 times and the answer is a crotchet (quarter note), it has the value of 1 and can fit into a semibreve 4 times.

Let's look at some diagrams of time signatures below as mentioned 4/4 is the most common time signature.

Type Of Beat	Duple Time	Triple Time	Quadruple Time
Crotchet Beat	2/4 ♩ ♩	3/4 ♩ ♩ ♩	4/4 ♩ ♩ ♩ ♩
Minim Beat	2/2 ♩ ♩	3/2 ♩ ♩ ♩	4/2 ♩ ♩ ♩ ♩
Quaver Beat	2/8 ♪ ♪	3/8 ♪ ♪ ♪	4/8 ♪ ♪ ♪ ♪

Now you can get sixteenth notes and so on, but for a beginner that isn't relevant. So, in the time signature I gave you of 4/4, the top number is how many beats in a bar, so what note from the diagram would you choose that can fit into that four times? Easy, the quarter note, or crotchet, depending whereabouts you're reading this.

So, remember, top number how many beats in a bar and bottom number the type of beat, so that is 4 quarter notes or crotches in a bar! Easy right? Now you'd be surprised how many people get confused about this.

CHORD PROGRESSIONS

Okay, one last thing to touch upon is chord progressions, so what is a chord progression? Well, a chord progression is a bunch of chords that are in the same key, or, as is commonly stated, "a bunch of chords that sound good together," they're just like a book—there's a beginning, a middle and an end and each chord you progress to is linking it to the final part or piece.

So, let's look at the notes in the key of C below.

C D E F G A B C

And before we start, most songs will begin with the first note of the key, also called the 'tonic', if you want to get fancy.

So, you're guaranteed in a chord progression in the key of C that every note apart from sharps or flats will sound good together, that's not to say you can't use sharps or flats, you'll have to be the judge of that by the tonal quality.

Although I've mentioned the c chord progression, the most common chord progression musicians stumble across is the g chord progression. I'll post an image down below

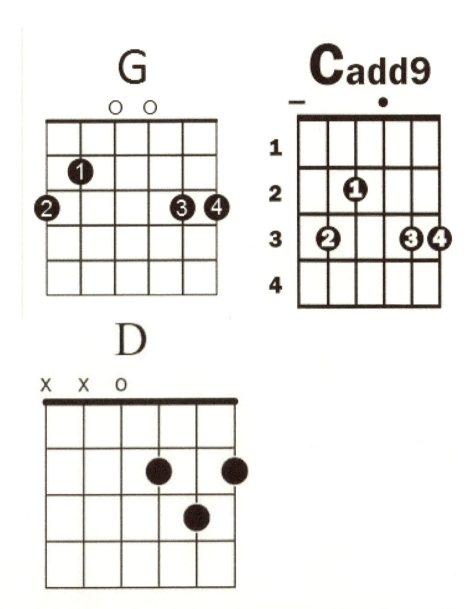

If you look at the G major Chord and the C Add 9 chord, you'll notice the chord is almost the same however you're lifting your 1st and 2nd fingers above a string per finger. If you practice these 3 chords you'll be able to play thousands of songs.

Now for a beginner guitarist I think we've pretty much covered it all.

Just too reiterate, you cannot become a master in a day, it will take years, but if you stick it out who knows? Maybe your name will be up with the greats one day.

Thanks for reading this book I hope this will make the road ahead a little clearer and good luck with your journey ahead.

(c) M Dibley 2014

CPSIA information can be obtained
at www.ICGtesting.com
Printed in the USA
BVHW042130010822
643598BV00008B/113